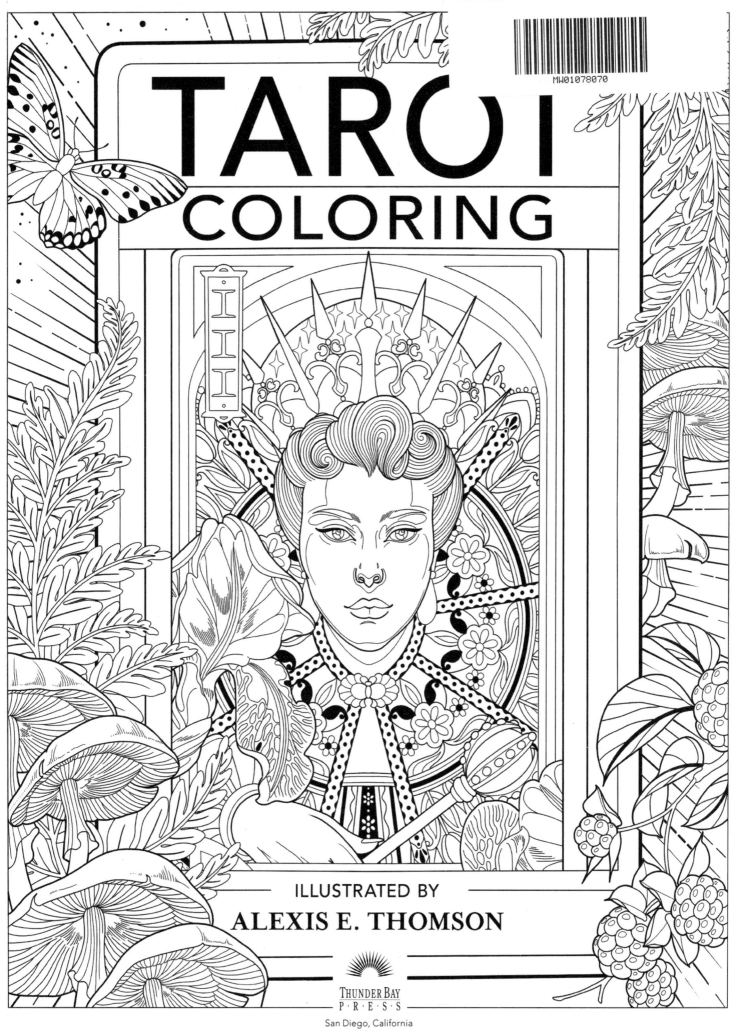

Written and edited by
Jocelyn Norbury

Designed by
Derrian Bradder

Cover design by
John Bigwood

Thunder Bay Press
An imprint of Printers Row Publishing Group
9717 Pacific Heights Blvd, San Diego, CA 92121
www.thunderbaybooks.com • mail@thunderbaybooks.com

First published in Great Britain in 2021 by LOM ART, an imprint of
Michael O'Mara Books Limited, 9 Lion Yard, Tremadoc Road, London SW4 7NQ

Printers Row Publishing Group is a division of
Readerlink Distribution Services, LLC.
Thunder Bay Press is a registered trademark of
Readerlink Distribution Services, LLC.

Correspondence regarding the content of this book should be sent
to Thunder Bay Press, Editorial Department, at the above address.
Author, illustration, and rights inquiries should be addressed to
Michael O'Mara Books Limited, 9 Lion Yard,
Tremadoc Road, London SW4 7NQ

Thunder Bay Press
Publisher: Peter Norton • Associate Publisher: Ana Parker
Acquisitions Editor: Kathryn C. Dalby

ISBN: 978-1-64517-903-0

Printed in China

25 24 23 22 21   1 2 3 4 5

Tarot decks come in many different styles. The beautiful natural and botanical imagery in this book has been created to convey the special significance of each card. The description opposite each design explores the elements included in the picture and how they relate to the card's meaning. There is also information about what the card would signify should you receive it in a reading.

The Tarot deck

The cards from the Major Arcana are all named and given a number from 0 to 21. Cards from the Minor Arcana are divided into four suits – Coins, Wands, Swords, and Cups. They are further sub-divided into number cards and face cards, similar to normal playing cards. In this book, the number cards have been omitted in order to focus on the more distinctive Ace and face cards.

How are Tarot cards used?

The Tarot can be a powerful tool for self-discovery and understanding. In a standard reading, the Tarot deck is shuffled by the receiver, then the practitioner lays out a number of the cards in a pattern known as a "spread." The meaning of each card shifts focus according to whether it is upright or reversed, its position in the spread, and the meaning of the other cards selected.

THE FOOL

Barnacle goslings, known for the death-defying, cliff-edge leaps they take soon after birth, act as a literal depiction of stepping into the unknown. The young geese, in their innocence, take this seemingly foolish action willingly and without fear, their purity of spirit reflected here by the rose icons in the card border. The dogwood flowers are a symbol of the loyalty and protection offered by man's best friend, who guards against fear of the unknown, while the mountains in the background represent challenges that will be encountered in the future, as yet unseen.

Upright:
Consider a step into the unknown as a step toward freedom and enlightening new experiences. The universe has a plan, and embracing it will open up a world of opportunity.

Reversed:
Everyone is liable to act foolishly on occasion, but dangerous consequences can be avoided by listening to intuition. If something seems too good to be true, it probably is.

THE MAGICIAN

Nature's ultimate magic trick – the transformation of caterpillar into butterfly – signifies new beginnings and the realization of hidden potential. Magical herbs include rosemary, to purify in preparation for this fresh start, as well as lavender and sage, known for their healing properties. Lilies, pictured in bloom, represent the blossoming of ideas and aspirations coming to fruition.

Upright:

Uniting the four elements and the four suits of the Minor Arcana, this card highlights the presence of all the resources required to manifest true intention. The Magician offers encouragement to forge ahead with an idea that has significant potential.

Reversed:

A harbinger of change, this card may indicate that potential remains unfulfilled. The inverted Magician is a master of manipulation and could be a sign that all is not what it seems.

THE MAGICIAN

THE HIGH PRIESTESS

A symbol of the divine feminine, the High Priestess
is surrounded by pomegranates, representing beauty,
fertility, and abundance. Along with the crescent moon
icons, the fruit is a reminder of the fecund nature of
womanhood. The pillars on either side of the figure echo
those flanking the Hierophant, the male counterpart
to the High Priestess. They symbolize duality – of
masculinity and femininity, darkness and light, and
of the conscious and subconscious. This card reminds
us of the value of both existing simultaneously.

Upright:
The High Priestess is the guardian of the
unconscious world and may be prompting the
receiver to listen closely to their intuition and
to follow instinct over rationale.

Reversed:
A struggle to trust the inner voice may be the result of
overpowering external noise. A period of withdrawal
may be necessary in order to recalibrate and to
emerge with a new focus on what is right.

THE HIGH
PRIESTESS

THE EMPRESS

The Empress depicts a woman wearing an
Elizabethan-style collar. The embodiment of
beauty and femininity, her expression is serene,
her lush surroundings signifying a strong connection
with nature. She has close links to both the mystical
and the natural worlds. The twelve stars on her crown
represent both the twelve months of the year and
the twelve planets of the solar system.

Upright:

With her opulent robes and lavish jewels, the Empress is
a card connected with abundance. It calls on the receiver
to embrace their sensuality and revel in the fruitfulness
of the world around them. It is also one of the strongest
indicators that a pregnancy is on its way.

Reversed:

The card asks for self-care to be a priority: the receiver
should turn their loving power and energy inward,
rather than focusing it on others. This is an
essential way to recharge and heal.

THE EMPEROR

The masculine counterpart to the Empress, the bearded Emperor is a paragon of wisdom and experience. An imposing figure that commands respect, in one hand he holds the ankh, the Egyptian symbol of life. In the other rests an orb, which represents the globe and therefore the Emperor's ultimate authority. A Chinese dragon, a traditional symbol of power and strength, encircles the card, emphasizing the incredible influence this Emperor wields. The ram head icons symbolize his connection with the astrological sign of Aries.

Upright:
A born leader, the receiver plays a protective role to those around them, providing them with stability and security. The sharing of wisdom, perhaps in a mentor role, will be rewarded with tremendous loyalty.

Reversed:
This card in a spread may indicate the receiver is too rigid in their thinking, which is having a negative effect on them or the people around them. A more flexible approach could shift the balance from domineering to authoritative.

THE HIEROPHANT

The male counterpart to the High Priestess, the
Hierophant, in his three-tiered crown, rules over
three worlds: the conscious, the subconscious, and the
superconscious. While the cardinals around him
symbolize pure devotion, the Hierophant himself is
the bridge between the earthly and the spiritual worlds,
which are represented by the two pillars that flank him.
In his hand he holds a triple scepter, reinforcing
his religious status. The marriage bands signify
the traditional values that this card represents.

Upright:
The Hierophant encourages the exploration of spiritual
values, prompting the receiver to wholeheartedly
embrace previously neglected traditions or rituals
to create a fulfilling daily practice.

Reversed:
In a spread, the reversed card serves as a reminder
that all wisdom can be found within. The receiver
should have the self-belief to follow their own path,
even if that means challenging the status quo.

THE LOVERS

These lovebirds represent unity and harmonious relationships. The flame flowers that surround them signify the passionate nature of a loving union, and the bleeding hearts are symbolic of honest expression. The apple icons and the snake weaving through the lush florals bring to mind the Garden of Eden, and symbolize the distractions that might be offered up by temptations of the flesh.

Upright:
The Lovers celebrates meaningful connections and open communication. In the face of a moral dilemma, the appearance of this card encourages a steadfastness of belief and the conviction to stand by what is right; in other words, to "choose love."

Reversed:
This card in a spread could indicate a disconnect within a close relationship or a struggle for inner harmony. It brings to the fore the importance of self-love, particularly in the face of difficult decisions.

THE CHARIOT

Under the celestial influence of the six-pointed stars in the background, the horse steers the chariot with strength and determination. The flowering roses that surround it show that the animal is grounded by the earth element. The crescent moons on the horse's tunic indicate something about to come into being, with the presence of alchemical symbols indicating that this may be a spiritual transformation.

Upright:
This card could signify the start of a journey that demands the receiver take control of their destiny. Confidence and focus are essential partners in overcoming obstacles.

Reversed:
This card may bring to light a lack of direction or drive, or highlight the limiting quality of self-doubt.

THE CHARIOT

STRENGTH

The masterful tiger showcases a raw, wild energy that is an essential and natural part of every living being. In contrast, the mountains in the background are symbolic of calm and stability. The two shown together indicate that intrinsic power must be tamed in order for it to be channeled for good. The infinity symbol, depicted in the card border, represents limitless potential and wisdom, while bamboo, one of nature's strongest materials, reinforces the central theme of the card.

Upright:
This card shines a light on the inner strength of the receiver. Directing compassion inward is encouraged in order to master anxieties and live courageously.

Reversed:
Fear and low self-esteem can be paralyzing. This card encourages a period of withdrawal in order to bring confidence back into balance.

THE HERMIT

The hermit crab, alone in its concealment, symbolizes the isolation and introspection experienced on the road to self-discovery. A journey that must be embarked on independently, the path becomes clearer with each step. The Seal of Solomon, a symbol of wisdom, is represented by a six-pointed starfish.

Upright:

The Hermit calls upon the receiver to look inward for the answers to life's big questions. It extends an invitation to shift focus to the inner world and to re-evaluate personal goals.

Reversed:

This card may suggest an excess of isolation, self-inflicted or otherwise. An effort to reconnect, inwardly or outwardly, may be beneficial.

THE WHEEL OF FORTUNE

One of the most symbolic cards of the Major Arcana, the Wheel of Fortune depicts a decorative wheel with the alchemical symbols for mercury, water, sulphur, and salt. Combined with the symbols for the four elements, this represents the formative power of these "building blocks" of life. The letters TORA, featured as part of the wheel design, are thought to be a version of Torah, meaning "law," and point to wisdom and self-understanding. Read the other way, TARO, they are an alternative spelling for Tarot. The sphinx cat, one paw raised like a Maneki Neko, represents knowledge and power. The elegant, open blooms are lotus flowers, symbolic of karma and the idea that "what goes around, comes around" – one of the central principles of the Wheel of Fortune.

Upright:
The wheel of fortune is always in motion, and this card serves to remind the receiver that life, too, is in a constant state of flux. Both good and bad fortune will feature – this card acts as a prompt to cherish the positive moments when they come around.

Reversed:
The receiver may be about to fall victim to an unforeseen circumstance or experience disappointment. Alternatively, it could be a sign that a negative cycle will be broken.

THE WHEEL OF
FORTUNE

JUSTICE

This card depicts an elaborate set of scales, the balance of the plates symbolizing the balance between the heart and the head. The ostrich feathers call to mind the ancient Egyptian goddess of truth and justice, Ma'at, who would weigh a person's heart after death against an ostrich feather, to determine if that person had led a virtuous life. The double-edged swords in the border signify that actions have consequences – everyone's path is determined by the decisions they make.

Upright:
For better or worse, all decisions will face judgement. The receiver must keep in mind that their actions affect both themselves and others, and they should be willing to be held accountable when the time comes.

Reversed:
The future depends on actions taken in the present. By letting go of guilt for past behavior, focus will shift in favor of taking decisive action for a more positive future.

THE HANGED MAN

The fruit bat swings peacefully from a branch, its upside-down pose providing it with an alternative view of the world. Surrounded by wisteria, a symbol of expanding consciousness, the Hanged Man highlights the importance of surrender in the quest for enlightenment.

Upright:

The Hanged Man calls on the receiver to take pause in order to recognize and break old patterns. The universe will provide a different perspective if you surrender to its will.

Reversed:

This card symbolizes a reluctance to change that may lead to missed opportunities. Relax expectations; what's meant to be, will be.

THE
HANGED MAN

DEATH

Death is one of the most feared cards in the deck, and indeed the skull, hooded like the Grim Reaper, reminds us of our mortality. Chrysanthemums, often given as a token of grief or bereavement, depicted alongside a raven and a death's-head moth, also appear ominous. However, Death is as much about new beginnings as endings, and comes with positive links to transformation and rebirth. The Tudor roses in the border represent purity and immortality, as well as commemorating the beauty that can be found in death as a part of life.

Upright:

Counterintuitively, Death can be one of the most positive cards in the deck. It signifies moving on from something that no longer serves us, in order to take advantage of fresh opportunities.

Reversed:

The Death card, reversed, can signify that resistance to change is preventing positive action and causing feelings of stagnation. A purge of the past may be necessary in order to move forward.

TEMPERANCE

This card is primarily concerned with balance. The chalices mixing water with wine represent the duality between the conscious and subconscious minds. The crown emblems in the border indicate the importance of taking a higher path in pursuit of life's true meaning.

Upright:

When life feels stressful or chaotic, keeping a sense of composure is paramount. Patience will help the receiver to reach their goals as long as they are also guided by a strong sense of purpose.

Reversed:

A period of excess needs to be balanced out. Moderation is the key to healing and will help equilibrium to be restored.

THE DEVIL

Representing the darker side of humanity, the goat pictured on this card is a reference to Baphomet – the half-man, half-goat symbol of the opposition between good and evil, male and female, human and animal. The open, leathery bat wings in the border are a nod to the traditional depiction of the devil. Pentagrams, too, are an emblem of the darker side of the occult, while chains are suggestive of oppression and a loss of personal power.

Upright:

Hedonism, lust, and materialism may provide short-term pleasure but are unlikely to result in long-term fulfillment. The power to break destructive patterns comes from acknowledging the influence they wield.

Reversed:

The receiver may be experiencing anxiety around letting go of unhealthy beliefs and behavior patterns. The Devil invites them to eliminate harmful influences to take control of their path.

THE DEVIL

THE TOWER

On the surface, the tower may appear solid, but a single lightning strike is enough to compromise its stability. A "castle built on sand," it is symbolic of ambition based on false premise. A lightning bolt – a sudden burst of energy – is depicted knocking off the top, or "crown," of the building, allowing this powerful energy from the universe to flow downward through it. Fireweed flowers bloom prolifically around the tower – these plants are often among the first to grow back on burned ground, and as such, represent the potential for transformation.

Upright:
The Tower is about expecting the unexpected.
A change or awakening is on the cards, possibly the result of external factors such as a past deception coming to light. This shift may feel painful, even destructive, but is for the greater good.

Reversed:
A precursor to change that comes from within, the Tower is a sign that planning ahead and heeding intuition will be necessary in order to minimize the destruction that this card foreshadows.

THE TOWER

THE STAR

Just as the scarab beetle navigates its path by the Milky Way, the Star provides a signpost out of a tumultuous time. A highly symbolic card, the two water jug icons represent the conscious and the subconscious mind, while the flowing water nourishes the earth, providing essential sustenance. Seven large, bright stars are symbolic of the seven chakras, and the five arms of the galaxy represent the five senses.

Upright:

The Star promises renewed faith after a period of destruction. A hopeful card that facilitates personal growth, it is a sign to "reach for the stars" to discover a new sense of purpose. A profound transformation is on its way that will bring huge rewards when embraced with an open heart.

Reversed:

This card may suggest the receiver is struggling to see the positive in the dramatic changes taking place. A period of self-care may help to renew energy reserves and accept that the universe is sending a life lesson rather than a punishment.

THE MOON

The Moon, a symbol of intuition, dreams, and the subconscious, is pictured alongside the beautiful luna moth, representing rebirth and regeneration. The large, flute-like moonflowers, too, are often associated with rejuvenation and renewal of the spirit. The dog motif, accompanied by a howling wolf, together represent both the tamed and wild elements of the unconscious mind.

Upright:
The Moon encourages the receiver to let go of fears from past experiences that might be preventing positive progression. Tune in to the power of the moon by setting intentions with the new moon, then using the lunar calendar to chart their progress.

Reversed:
Working through fears and anxieties can be liberating but also intimidating. Instead of pushing deep feelings aside, trust that heeding the inner voice will provide clarity and direction.

THE SUN

The sun shines its bright, life-giving energy on the
bee, a symbol of light and warmth, and a wheatfield,
representing nourishment. A card that is closely
linked to purity of spirit and optimism, the child
icons within the frame represent innocence.
The four open sunflowers symbolize the four
suits of the Minor Arcana as well as the
four elements – earth, water, fire, and air.

Upright:
This card highlights that the receiver is simply glowing
with happiness and positivity. Their warmth and energy
are irresistable to others. The Sun encourages them to
shine their light on those closest to them.

Reversed:
Unfortunate setbacks or unexpected pitfalls
may have hampered enthusiasm, but trust that this
is a temporary state. Let go of worries and concerns
and simply have fun to reawaken the child inside.

THE SUN

JUDGEMENT

The phoenix rises from the ashes to the sound of a trumpet call, its rebirth symbolizing the final journey to meet the creator. The rolling clouds in the background remind us that the judgement of the universe hangs over all of our actions and that this appraisal is inevitable. Sakura, or cherry blossoms, symbolize renewal, and there are echoes of the Death card in the acknowledgment that every ending is also a new beginning.

Upright:

Self-evaluation plays an important role in personal growth, and a sudden awakening may be prompted by the realization that previous actions may have had a permanent impact on the path ahead.

Reversed:

Harsh, self-inflicted judgements from the past may have resulted in a paralyzing lack of self-belief. Forgiveness will enable the receiver to learn important lessons, heal, and move forward with confidence.

JUDGEMENT

THE WORLD

A Yggdrasil tree, which in Norse cosmology means "world's tree," grows strong and sturdy, its roots encircling the globe on which it stands. A fern, itself a symbol of renewal, is depicted as a circular wreath, calling attention to the cyclical nature of life itself. It is complemented by a pair of Atlas moths which, due to their ability to transform during their life cycle, are often seen as a sign of rebirth.

Upright:

The receiver may be relishing a sense of accomplishment for a job well done. This card invites reflection on past achievements and encourages a spirit of gratitude for the rewards this brings. The World is sometimes a precursor to a period of travel.

Reversed:

Gaining closure on a past issue is necessary in order to live fully in the present. Goals are all within reach, but taking the quickest or easiest route may not result in complete satisfaction.

THE SUIT OF COINS

The Suit of Coins, also known as Pentacles, is associated with the earth element and, accordingly, the astrological signs of earth: Taurus, Virgo, and Capricorn. Just as the earth provides the foundations for all growth, this suit, too, is linked to nurture and support, with a further focus on reliability and responsibility.

This suit is primarily concerned with material matters – finances, work, and health. It is tied to the outer world and the effect that the receiver has on growth and progress within that world. Cards of this suit are also associated with ego and self-esteem.

A spread made up predominantly of Coins cards indicates issues around money, career, or other material concerns.

ACE OF COINS

A hand emerges from the clouds, offering up a coin to whoever is ready to take advantage of this good fortune. The Ace of Coins is a card primarily associated with abundance, the verdant roses and lilies indicating that opportunity is "ripe for the picking." Eucalyptus, sometimes referred to as the "silver dollar," acts as a symbol of material wealth.

Upright:

There are new opportunites on the horizon, most probably relating to finance, career, or health. The onus rests on the receiver, however, to turn opportunity into success. Through a combination of determination and effort, wealth and prosperity are within reach.

Reversed:

This card in a spread advises caution – careful planning and foresight are essential to ensure a lucky chance doesn't slip away. The receiver should keep in mind the proverb, "There's many a slip 'twixt the cup and the lip."

KING OF COINS

The strong, regal bull is a born leader, a physical representation of ambition and success. This animal, unafraid to flaunt its achievements, shows off a crown decorated with grapes and vines – a celebration of material wealth and plentitude. The trees and flowers that surround this noble beast include the king protea, emphasizing the majestic and stately nature of the card's central figure.

Upright:

The receiver would be wise to gather their resources and channel their energies into the pursuit of an ultimate goal, because the King of Coins indicates that success and fulfillment are well within reach.

Reversed:

Impatience and overindulgence can undermine the power and authority of even the most prosperous king. Self-discipline is a useful tool in managing relationships with money and wealth.

QUEEN OF COINS

The Queen of Coins is surrounded by flowers, spilling over with the lushness of the natural world. It is difficult to overlook her relationship with Mother Earth, and with it her association with fertility, richness, and sensual pleasure. As a woodland fairie queen she is in perfect harmony with her environment, indicating that all aspects of life are in balance.

Upright:
Nurturing and caring, the Queen of Coins in a spread suggests that finding the ideal balance between work and home life can be achieved by integrating both elements as much as possible, without foregoing independence.

Reversed:
A short break away from the demands of work and family may be enough to reset and re-energize. Prioritize self-care and the benefits will be seen across all areas of life.

QUEEN OF COINS

KNIGHT OF COINS

The stag, wearing a suit of decorative armor, rears up in order to assess the path ahead. In his state of quiet determination he is set on reaching an ultimate destination, but rather than rushing headlong into action, applies a practical, deliberate energy to the mission.

Upright:

Trustworthy and reliable, diligent and tenacious, the Knight of Coins reinforces the message that putting effort into even the most mundane tasks, perhaps sticking with tried and tested methods, is sometimes the most effective route to success.

Reversed:

This card may be a sign that the receiver is stuck in a rut and craving a change of scenery. Taking some responsibilities too seriously may have a knock-on effect on other areas of life. A better balance is called for to avoid a physical or emotional burnout.

KNIGHT OF COINS

PAGE OF COINS

Chickadees were considered by Native Americans to be messengers of good fortune, and so this bird, a missive held in its beak, offers the promise of growth and opportunity. The Page's strong connection to the earth is symbolized by the pine tree on which the bird perches. The mushrooms, growing as they do from decayed matter, are a sign that something can be cultivated from nothing. The Page of Coins may not be blessed with abundance currently, but is a master of finding opportunity for growth in unlikely places.

Upright:

This card is a positive sign for a new venture. The ability to manifest ambition into success, however, is reliant on good sense and pragmatism.

Reversed:

The receiver may wish to take their time to get a new project off the ground, or might be concerned about repeating past mistakes. This card acts as a reminder that the very act of learning from a failure can reframe it as a success.

THE SUIT OF WANDS

The Suit of Wands is associated with the fire element. Like fire, it can be either creative or destructive and is often volatile. Cards of this suit are associated with energy and passion, as well as ambition and inspiration.

Fire is a masculine element that has links to the astrological signs of Leo, Sagittarius, and Aries. Wands cards deal with the spiritual aspect of consciousness and the values at the core of our being that drive us to reach our full potential.

A number of Wands cards appearing in a spread can be a sign that the receiver is seeking a greater purpose in life and is looking for direction to help them discover their inner motivations.

ACE OF WANDS

A wand, grasped firmly by a hand, occupies
the center of the card, the young leaves sprouting
from it signifying unlimited potential for growth.
The castle in the background, in its grandeur, symbolizes
opportunities that are to come; however the flames serve
to highlight that the path will not be without obstacles.

Upright:

A card that offers up pure potential, the Ace of Wands
gives the receiver all the encouragement they need to
follow their heart and pursue their dreams. A creative
hobby promises the opportunity for personal growth.

Reversed:

Enthusiasm may be abundant, but without clear
direction, motivation can quickly dwindle. Homing
in on true passions can reignite inspiration.

ACE OF WANDS

KING OF WANDS

This regal lion is wearing a crown decorated with salamanders – both the big cat and the lizard are traditional symbols of fire and strength. The salamanders, also associated with transformation, are depicted biting their own tails and represent not only the infinite nature of opportunity but also the act of pushing through obstacles. The fire-breathing dragons symbolize a powerful, masculine energy.

Upright:
A card brimming with optimistic energy, the King of Wands reminds the receiver to keep focus – to define their goals and work tirelessly toward achieving them. A combination of intentions and hard work is essential for prosperity.

Reversed:
The receiver should be mindful that confidence can easily descend into arrogance, and there is a fine line between an assertive leader and an overbearing bully.

KING of WANDS

QUEEN OF WANDS

This devil queen's proud, direct gaze is testament to her deep self-assurance, while her horned headpiece suggests that she is also in touch with her darker side. She wears a suit of elaborate body armor, which, along with the fiery torches in the background, symbolize her strength and resilience.

Upright:

The Queen of Wands encourages the receiver to be bold, own their power, and believe in themselves and what they stand for. Energy, passion, and enthusiasm are the key to creating positive change.

Reversed:

Confidence doesn't always come from being the life and soul of the party. Self-respect grows from the inside out, so stepping back and taking time to reconnect with the inner voice is essential.

QUEEN OF WANDS

KNIGHT OF WANDS

The rhino – fearless, determined, and powerful with his armored horn – roams the hot, barren plains of the savanna. His snort tells us he is full of energy and ready for action. The belching, cauldron-like volcanoes that surround him provide echoes of the fiery theme of all cards in the Suit of Wands.

Upright:

The Knight of Wands indicates that the receiver possesses all of the strength and enthusiasm required to pursue new opportunites. Passion, energy, and charisma go a long way toward making dreams a reality.

Reversed:

Passion and energy without direction can result in feelings of restlessness. Overcompensating for this by taking on too much can result in physical or emotional burnout. Taking a breath and trying a more single-minded approach could be beneficial.

KNIGHT OF WANDS

PAGE OF WANDS

The hawk, with its legendary associations with fire, is also a symbol of freedom. Glowing lanterns light the path ahead, but this Page is only just embarking on his journey. The purpose of his mission is made apparent by the quill pen, which indicates he is eager to spread his message far and wide. Fireflies and lightning represent the fire element.

Upright:

A wonderful creative energy is flowing, but the appearance of this card in a spread indicates that taking time to think things through fully, before embarking on a journey of discovery, is advisable.

Reversed:

Forcing ideas into fruition before they are fully formed may be detrimental to their outcome. Giving them a little space to breathe may be helpful.

THE SUIT OF SWORDS

The Suit of Swords is associated with the air element, and deals with matters of the mind and intellect, particularly logic, attitudes, and belief systems.

Air is a masculine element that, although invisible, can have a big impact. As such, the meanings of cards in the Swords suit are linked to communication, courage, curiosity, and fairness. Less positively, they can also indicate anger, ruthlessness, and judgement.

Should a reading reveal mostly Swords cards, it is a sign that struggle and conflict are affecting the receiver. They may be seeking resolution, but there is a strong need for decisive action rather than analysis.

ACE OF SWORDS

A hand wields an upright sword balancing a heavily embellished crown. Together, they represent a mental breakthrough or a new clarity of thought. The laurel wreath that surrounds the crown is traditionally a symbol of victory and achievement. Forbidding-looking mountains predict challenges to come, while soft, fluffy clouds in the background represent the divine.

Upright:
With an open, receptive mind and fresh ideas bubbling to the surface, now is the perfect time to concentrate intellectual energy on a new project. The Ace of Swords provides the motivation, but the receiver will need to channel it effectively in order to succeed.

Reversed:
Forcing an idea into being before it is fully formed can be counterproductive. Taking time to set clear goals and make defined plans can be a more useful route to gaining inner clarity.

KING OF SWORDS

The regal peacock, with its feathers a brilliant blue, is symbolic of a quest for spiritual enlightenment. The emperor dragonflies represent not only change and transformation but also self-realization – the knowledge that to understand something on an intellectual level is not always enough. The clouds appear settled and still, signifying the importance of calmness and clarity of thought over sweeping, dramatic change.

Upright:
This card in a spread suggests that the receiver possesses an aptitude for clear, logical, and well-balanced reasoning – the perfect qualities to navigate difficult decisions.

Reversed:
Quiet, understated authority can be a positive characteristic, but this card in a spread indicates it may be being used as a tool to manipulate. A lack of mental clarity may lead to procrastination and indecisiveness.

QUEEN OF SWORDS

The Queen of Swords directs her uncompromising gaze toward the receiver. Her angel wings and a halo-esque crown indicate that, despite this show of strength, she is in touch with her softer side. As well as being a nod to the air element, the appearance of butterflies suggests transformation and growth, and the clouds accumulating around the queen emphasize the ongoing nature of these changes – they are unlikely to blow through without making an impact.

Upright:

An upfront and honest approach can be intimidating, but beneath this uncompromising exterior there is a softer side, albeit one that seeks to connect with others on an intellectual, rather than emotional, level.

Reversed:

Clarity of vision combined with a direct manner can be perceived as coldness or lack of compassion. On the other hand, the appearance of this card could suggest that emotions are clouding usually clear judgement.

QUEEN OF SWORDS

KNIGHT OF SWORDS

The ibex, in his decorative armor, steps purposefully upward to reach the mountain peak. High up in the sky, the pure mountain air that the whiskeyjacks inhabit is symbolic of the pure spirit that drives the knight forward on his mission.

Upright:

Ambitious and focused, the receiver remains undeterred by any obstacles in their path. Inspired by the Knight of Swords, they should be assertive and single-minded in pursuit of their goals, while avoiding acting hastily or impulsively.

Reversed:

Restlessness, caused by an excess of energy without direction, can lead to frustration and impulsiveness. Finding an outlet for this energy will make for a more focused state of mind.

KNIGHT OF SWORDS

PAGE OF SWORDS

Swifts, which can stay aloft longer than any other birds, are pictured in flight and, alongside the soaring paper airplanes, bring a feeling of dynamism and energy to the card. There is a sense of positive movement, of action being taken and plans underway. The hot-air balloons are indicative of travel and new adventure, and suggest embracing curiosity about the world.

Upright:

The Page of Swords offers encouragement to embrace exciting plans for the future. Adopting alternative ways of thinking and communicating may benefit this spirit of adventure.

Reversed:

This card in a spread may be a sign that the receiver is reluctant to communicate openly and honestly. There is also a possibility that they have fallen into the trap of promising more than they can deliver.

PAGE of SWORDS

THE SUIT OF CUPS

This suit is concerned with feelings, love, relationships, and other emotional connections. With links to the water element, the cards represent intuition, healing, and cleansing. Symbolism within the suit emphasizes the power of water, whether soft and gentle, like lapping waves, or more forceful, like raging river rapids.

Associated with the astrological water signs of Pisces, Cancer, and Scorpio, cards in the Suit of Cups indicate the heart ruling the head, overwhelming emotions, or a preoccupation with fantasy and imagination.

A number of Cups cards in a spread can mean the receiver is seeking resolution for a conflict of the heart, is struggling with personal matters, or is experiencing issues around creativity.

ACE OF CUPS

The cup-like nautilus shell, a vessel that symbolizes the subconscious mind, is offered forth by an anonymous hand. It is overflowing with five streams, each representing one of the five senses. In keeping with a card that has spiritual fulfillment at its heart, the crashing waves embody the idea of abundant emotion and intuition. The dove feathers act as a tangible symbol of divine love, passing from the heavens down to earth.

Upright:

A fresh start is on the cards, one that offers the opportunity for emotional gratification. This card offers release from past hurt – an "emotional cleanse."

Reversed:

The overflowing cup has run dry, and the receiver is feeling an emotional emptiness or creative block. Focusing on self-love is an effective way to refill the cup and bring back a sense of flow.

KING OF CUPS

The killer whale, masterful "king of the sea," is depicted alongside a crown of bubbles, indicating his royal status. His immense strength and power mean that he keeps his course no matter how turbulent the sea becomes. Octopus tentacles, which represent emotional life, give the impression that this king is in touch with his feelings without being overcome by them.

Upright:
Acknowledging and accepting a full range of emotions while keeping a clear head is a skill. The King of Cups challenges the receiver to hold their boundaries, even when challenged.

Reversed:
In times of high emotion it is important to practice self-compassion. Try to bring emotional turbulence under control without resorting to repressing or ignoring feelings.

KING OF CUPS

QUEEN OF CUPS

Water is the home of emotions and intuition, represented here by a beautiful mermaid. Her hair, swirling gently in the calm sea, lends her an air of serenity. The tranquility of the water suggests that although she is in touch with her feelings, she does not allow them to overwhelm her. Angelfish symbolize the unconscious mind, and here the mermaid is able to perceive them objectively, reinforcing the idea that she is in control of her emotions.

Upright:
Kind, supportive, and nurturing to others, the receiver should turn their compassion inward, or seek out someone who will take care of them, rather than the other way around.

Reversed:
The receiver may be suffering from a lack of perspective regarding their emotional health. They may be either repressing their feelings or allowing them to take over. Taking a step back can help to regain a sense of perspective.

QUEEN of CUPS

KNIGHT OF CUPS

Traditionally seen as a symbol of strength and power, the seahorse moves slowly, radiating calm and a quiet grace. A gentle, compassionate nature defines the Knight of Cups, who is led by the heart and seeks to spread a sense of peace to others. Adding to the underwater scene, the tropical fish and ornate shells represent the sea, which is often linked to imagination and creativity.

Upright:
Beauty and creativity are the life force of the Knight of Cups. This card promotes following the heart over the head and listening to intuition in order to transform dreams into reality.

Reversed:
The receiver may feel their emotions or creativity are being stifled, leading to frustration. A less fanciful approach, ensuring that fantasies are grounded in reality, means they are more likely to come true.

KNIGHT of CUPS

PAGE OF CUPS

A great white pelican carries a message in its beak. Fish, traditionally symbols of creativity and intuition, weave in and out of lotus flowers, bringing hope that inspiration can make an appearance when least expected. These flowers, which flourish in less than perfect conditions, prove that beauty can spring from unexpected places.

Upright:

Inspiration strikes out of the blue. Embracing creative intuition and remaining open to new ideas is the key to unlocking life's fullest potential. Anything is possible.

Reversed:

A period of creative block may be caused by self-doubt. Inspiration can be rekindled by listening to intuition and focusing on whatever brings joy.

PAGE of CUPS

The History of Tarot

The first Tarot cards were invented in Italy in the fifteenth century and were designed to be used for parlor games. Based on a standard deck of cards with four suits, an additional 21 specially illustrated cards were added, and eventually the pack was separated into two groups, the Major and the Minor Arcana.

It wasn't until the eighteenth century that Tarot cards began to be used for mystical reasons, and the art has captivated people with its magic ever since. In order to tell fortunes, each card was ascribed a meaning based around astrology and the four elements. The first professional Tarot reader, Jean-Baptiste Alliette, wrote a guide to using the cards and created a system for Tarot reading that is used to this day.